Life
Can't Throw a
Fastball

A Guide to Personal Finance

MICHAEL D. A. BAKER

PAGE PUBLISHING
Conneaut Lake, PA

First originally published by Page Publishing 2020

ISBN 978-1-6624-1380-3 (pbk)
ISBN 978-1-6624-1381-0 (digital)

Printed in the United States of America

Introduction

If you are like most people, money plays a major role in your life. You may live paycheck to paycheck. You may do much better than that, but life seems to throw you its fair share of financial curveballs. And many people have no idea where all the money they make goes. If you want a better handle on your money, as well as help with the major money issues in your life, this book was written for you.

Another reason I wrote this book is that people should not have to learn about personal finance the hard way, by making mistakes and then learning from them. By reading this book, you will learn the things you need to know, without having to make the mistakes.

CHAPTER 1

Two Hundred Dollars Can Change Your Life

Life is full of financial curveballs. You may get a flat tire, a speeding ticket or a parking ticket, or your car may have a dead battery. Or you make have a financial emergency that has nothing to do with your car. If you do not have two hundred dollars set aside for such emergencies, what do you do? You put the cost of the new car battery, or whatever the emergency is, on a credit card.

When the credit card bill comes, you do not have enough money to pay the bill in full, so you make a small payment—enough to cover the minimum amount due—and your credit card balance starts to rise. Only 1 percent of people pay their credit card bill in full when it arrives in the mail or online. If you had an emergency fund of two hundred dollars, you could pay the bill in full, and not only would your credit card balance not rise, but you would not incur interest charges on your credit card. This is how two hundred dollars can change your life. No stressing out over life's unexpected financial surprises, no credit card balances, and no interest charges on your credit cards. Many credit cards charge 18 percent interest a year or more. The interest charges on a credit card can really add up quickly. So the first step in getting control of your finances is to have an emergency fund of two hundred dollars.

You need to have this two hundred dollars at all times because you never know when a financial emergency will occur. If one does, use some or all of your two hundred dollars to pay off the bill. Then you need a plan to replenish your emergency fund. Say your plan is to save twenty-five dollars a week. If you get paid once every two weeks, put aside fifty dollars per paycheck or twenty-five a week to start building up your emergency fund until you have two hundred again. If you don't have two hundred dollars in savings now, start setting money aside until you do have two hundred. Twenty-five dollars a week for eight weeks will get you to two hundred.

A Christmas Club Account

A Christmas club account is an account you open at a bank or credit union, putting money aside every week or every paycheck. Then right before Thanksgiving, you take your money out so you can spend it on Christmas presents, starting on Black

Friday. The advantages are that you save money all year round, earn some interest on your money, then have the money in time for Christmas season at the stores.

Very few people have Christmas club accounts, however. So what do they do? Most put the presents they purchase at Christmas time on a credit card. Then they spend the next year paying off that amount. When November rolls around, they have almost paid the amount off in full. That is the good news. The bad news is that Black Friday is just a few weeks away. Then they start the process all over again, charging presents to the credit card. So they always have a credit card balance and are always paying high credit card interest charges.

A Christmas club account is a way to break the credit card cycle, to have money saved up so you can use cash or a debit card instead of a credit card for purchases. Each year, you get your money and spend it on presents, knowing you are not increasing the balances on your credit cards.

Please note: a Hanukkah account or Kwanzaa account is the same thing as a Christmas club account.

Living Paycheck to Paycheck

How many times have you seen a car on the road with a doughnut tire? A doughnut tire is a small tire used when one of the regular tires on your car goes flat. There are only two reasons you should see a doughnut tire on a car. The first is if a person just had a flat tire, put on the doughnut tire, and is driving to the tire shop. The other, more common reason, is that a car had a flat tire and the owner does not have the seventy dollars to purchase a new tire. A doughnut tire can last a few thousand miles, so the car's owner drives on it until he or she gets paid again and can afford a new full-size tire.

So if you see a doughnut tire on a car, the odds are that the person driving the car does not have enough money for a new tire and is living paycheck to paycheck. A lot more people than you think are living paycheck to paycheck. So an emergency fund and a budget are very important.

No Interest and No Payments for Two Years!

Things are advertised all the time with no interest and no payments for two years. For example, you can buy an entire set of furniture for the family room, including a sofa, love seat, recliner, and coffee table. With the exception of the coffee table, everything is leather. And it can be yours for just 1,999 dollars. You make no payments and no interest for two years. Yes, no money down!

It sounds like you can make no payments for two years, then start making your payments. But if you read the fine print, you have to be finished paying the entire balance off in two years, or the seller goes back to the date of purchase and charges you 28 percent from that day on, until you finish paying off the balance. That means the 1,999-dollar family room can end up costing you more than 3,000 dollars, or even more if you don't pay off the balance quickly. *Ouch!* This nasty little trick of going retro on you has even been written into the language of some gym memberships.

So if you find yourself in one of these situations and the two years are about to end—and you don't have the money to pay off the balance in full—what should you do? Go to a credit union or bank immediately! Get a loan for the balance that you owe, and pay off the balance before the two years are up. The credit union or the bank won't go retro on you. It can only charge you interest starting with day you take out the loan. Getting a loan will save you thousands of dollars in interest charges.

What if your credit is so bad that no bank or credit union will loan you the money? Then use a credit card check and pay off the balance that way. The credit card company will start charging you interest from the date on the check and not go retro on you back to the date that you purchased the family room set.

CHAPTER 2

Sticking to a Budget

The first step in making a budget is to get a pad of lined paper. Start with the first of the month. Pick a month that is an average month for you. Record all the money that comes in for the month, and record all the money you spend that month. Each night before you go to bed, record what you spent that day. It is not good enough to record that you got sixty dollars out of the ATM. You have to record that you spent twenty dollars on gas for your car and forty dollars on food from the grocery store. This is the level of detail that is needed. Do this each day for the entire month. You also have to record bills that are paid automatically from your checking or savings account.

Once the month has ended, start putting what you spent into categories, such as gas for your car, food, the phone bill, internet service, television, restaurants, movies, and so on.

What if you pay a bill annually or semiannually in a month other than your budget month?

Let's say you pay your auto insurance premium annually every February, and your budget month is May. You would show no charges in May for auto insurance. This would cause your budget to be wrong, because you really spent more than would be shown for the month. Take your auto insurance premium and divide it by twelve, and add that amount as an expense to your May budget.

What if you pay a bill annually or semiannually in your budget month? Now you have to take that bill and divide it by twelve if you pay annually or by six if you pay semiannually, and only deduct that amount from your May budget. If you don't do this, you would be showing too much expense in the month of May.

You also need to make adjustments for special purchases. Let's say you purchased some patio furniture in May, your budget month, and it cost three hundred dollars. You don't buy patio furniture every month. You might only make a purchase like this once a year. If so, divide the three-hundred-dollar patio furniture bill by twelve, and only show a twenty-five-dollar expense for the month of May. Now your budget more accurately reflects what your expenses will be like on a monthly basis.

If You Come Up Short

Say you recorded all your revenue and expenses for the month, and you made all the adjustments described above for items that you pay for annually or semiannually, as well as your special purchases. But you discover that your outflows (purchases) exceed your inflows (revenue) by two hundred dollars a month. What should you do?

This 200-dollar shortage is a serious problem. It means you will be putting 2,400 dollars a year, plus interest, on your credit cards. If nothing changes, you will be putting 200 dollars a month on your credit card every month, every year. In 10 years, you will have 24,000 dollars in credit card debt, plus interest! You could be more than 30,000 in the hole! What you need to do is find a way to save 200 dollars a month to prevent this from happening.

Go over each category of your expenses to see where you can save money. You might have to eat out less. One solution might be to bring a bag lunch instead of going out to eat at lunchtime. Do you really need all those premium channels on your television bill? Can you join Costco or another discount store to save money on your purchases? Maybe you have to rent movies from Redbox at $1.59 a night as opposed to renting movies from your television set at $5.99 for the same movie. Really look at each category carefully and see what you are spending your money on. What are you willing to give up or cut down on, and what are you not willing to give up?

These are important questions, and everyone will answer them differently.

Paying your auto and homeowner's insurance bills annually or semiannually is usually cheaper than paying monthly. And having your auto and home-owner's insurance with the same company usually saves you money because most companies have a multipolicy discount. It's also a good idea to shop your auto insurance. Call three or four well-known companies, and compare apples-to-apples coverage to see which company is cheaper. You might be able to save thirty to fifty dollars a month. Also remember to get a quote that includes your homeowner's or renter's insurance to get a multipolicy discount.

What are you paying monthly for your phone bill? Shop to see if you can get a better deal with another company. Sometimes just calling your existing phone company and seeing if it has a better plan will save you money.

Buying for Less

K-Cups for coffee cost less at Walmart than at your local grocery store. Costco takes two boxes of cereal and glues them together. It then sells them for less than your local grocery store. All this saved money really adds up. And you are purchasing the same items. You are just spending less money to buy them.

You must have the attitude that no matter what it takes, you will find a way to save two hundred dollars a month, so you are not spending more money than you are making. In the vast majority of cases, you can save the two hundred a month without having to take drastic steps, such as getting a roommate or moving to a smaller place.

CHAPTER 3

Getting Out of Debt

Let's say you have the following credit card debt:

Card	Amount of debt	Budgeted amount per month
Exxon	$ 200	$ 50
Home Depot	$ 800	$100
Visa	$2,000	$150
MasterCard	$3,100	$200
Total	$6,100	$500

You are 6,100 dollars in debt in this example, and you are paying 500 dollars a month on your credit cards. Here is an easy way to get out of debt, and it's pain-free!

First, stop using your credit cards, so the balances stop increasing. If you want to buy something, use your debit card.

Next, have a garage or lawn sale to get rid of some things you no longer need or want, including things you have not used in a long time. Price everything very reasonably, so the items sell. Let's say you rake in 100 dollars from your garage sale. Use the whole 100 dollars plus your normal 50 dollars to apply 150 dollars to the Exxon bill. Your balance is now down to 50 dollars. Next month, you will pay off this bill in full.

Just like with a diet, people like to see results quickly, or they lose interest. You just paid off one bill. More bills will be paid off very soon. As soon as you pay off the Exxon bill, apply the 50 dollars a month that you were paying on the Exxon bill to the next-lowest bill, in this case the Home Depot bill. You are now paying 150 dollars a month on the Home Depot bill. What you are creating is a financial snowball. At 100 dollars a month, it would take eight months to pay off the Home Depot bill. (I am ignoring interest in this example because I am illustrating a concept.) At 150 dollars a month, it will take only six months from the time you started paying off your credit cards to pay off the Home Depot bill in full!

Just as soon as the Home Depot bill is paid off, use the one hundred dollars you were paying on it and the fifty dollars you were paying on the Exxon bill, and add that to the amount you are paying on the Visa bill. You are now paying three hundred dollars a month on the Visa bill! Yes, as soon as the Visa bill is paid off in full, you will be paying five hundred dollars on the MasterCard bill. When you are paying five hundred on one credit card and not increasing its balance, the card is paid off very quickly!

Many people will tell you that to save the most money in interest charges, you should pay off the card with the highest interest rate first. But I have noticed something about people: they want to see results quickly, or some people go back to their old ways of running up the credit card balances. By paying off the Exxon credit card in the previous example, you started the financial snowball quickly and saw results quickly. Once people start to see results, they are more likely to stick with the plan and continue paying off their credit card balances.

How long did it take you to pay off all your credit cards with this method? Exactly one year! You were not asked to tighten your belt and do without, and all your credit cards now have zero balances. You now have a five-hundred-dollar surplus in your budget every month!

CHAPTER 4

Using Credit Cards Wisely

Almost everyone has credit cards. They are very help-ful when purchasing airfare and many other things. But what happens when the bill comes? It's hard to believe, but only 1 percent of people pay their bal-ance in full! The other 99 percent pay interest on their credit cards. That's the real reason so many credit cards offer airline miles and other benefits to use their card. They make a ton of interest on your unpaid balance. Some credit cards charge 1.5 percent interest a month on your unpaid balance. That's 18 percent interest a year. Many credit cards charge even higher rates. Over time, the interest charges on your unpaid balance will add up to thousands of dollars.

If you are late with a payment or miss a payment on your credit card, your interest rate will go up a lot, to 28 percent or more. Some cards won't increase your interest rate after your first late payment. But don't be late or miss a payment a second time, or your interest rate will go up. Your credit score will also be lowered. If you are ever late or accidently miss a payment, contact your credit card company. Given your good history of making payments, they might not raise your rate the first time. So you have everything to gain by calling.

Making the Most of Free Money

Let's assume you have a zero balance on your credit card, and you make a purchase with it. Then the bill comes. If you pay the bill in full so you go back to a zero balance, you will not be charged any interest. So such a thing as free money does exist.

But what if you are like the vast majority of people and you have a balance on your credit card when you make that purchase? Well, then your credit card company will start charging you interest on that purchase from the day of the purchase! And you will continue to pay interest until you pay off your credit card and get your balance to zero.

The Pitfalls of 0 Percent Cards

Many people think credit cards are not a problem. They will just get a credit card that has a 0 percent introductory offer, and when the 0 percent rate is about to end, they will transfer their balance to another 0 percent credit card. The plan sounds great, until something goes wrong. If life throws you one if its curveballs and you lose your job, or something else happens and you no longer qualify for a 0 percent card, the plan falls apart. Everything is based on ratios. Your income and the amount of your debt determines your debt ratio. If your debt ratio gets high enough, you might not qualify for a 0 percent credit card, and you will be stuck with the credit card that you have and the interest rate on that card once the 0 percent rate has ended. So the amount of credit card debt that you have does matter, and if it grows large enough, it is a problem.

When a Purchase Pushes You Over the Limit

Say you go to the store and decide to purchase something. When you check out, you use your credit card. Your card is approved, so you take your purchase and leave the store. But when you get your bill, you discover that you are over your limit, and your credit card company charges you a fee. But it was your credit card company that approved your purchase.

Your credit card company knew that if it approved your purchase, that would put you over your limit, and then it could charge you an over-limit fee. As long as you are over your limit, you will continue to be charged an over-limit fee. So what can you do about this?

The first thing you can do is call your credit card company. Explain your situation, and ask that the over-limit fee be removed. Sometimes this will work. The longer you have been a customer with the credit card company and the more purchases you have made, the better your case. If the person you speak to does not agree to remove the over-limit fee, ask to speak with a manager. My philosophy in life is if you have nothing to lose, do it! Many times in life, ask yourself, "What is the worst that could happen?" In this case, the worst that can happen is that the manager says no. Well, that is the situation you are already in! So asking for the fee to be waived has no downside! That means you should definitely ask.

Even if the credit card company agrees to waive the fee, also ask that the credit limit on your card be raised. Once again, you have nothing to lose. In many cases, you can get your credit limit raised by five hundred dollars or one thousand dollars, just by asking. I am not telling you to get the credit limit on your card increased so you can go out and put more purchases on your card. I am asking you to get your credit card limit raised so you can put some distance between your current credit card balance and your credit limit. Then if you find yourself needing to make another fifty-dollar purchase, you won't be back in the situation you are in now, being over your limit and looking at paying over-limit fees.

What is the next thing you should do? Start paying down the balance on that credit card immediately. Life is unpredictable. The lower the balance you have on your card, the less you will be charged in interest charges, and the less chance you will go over your limit if you make a purchase with that card.

Paying Ten Dollars over the Minimum

Suppose you have a credit card with a zero balance. You go to the mall and purchase 1,000 dollars of necessities. Then you do not use your credit card again. Your credit card company requires a minimum payment of 2 percent, or 20 dollars, and your credit card interest is 1.5 percent a month. The interest you are charged is fifteen dollars. This means that if you make the minimum payment, your balance will only go down by $5, from $1,000 to $995! For budget purposes, you continue to make your 20-dollar payment each month. How long will it take you to pay off your credit card? Amazingly, the answer is 92 months! That is more than seven-and-a-half years. Over that time, you will have paid a total of $1,840. That is 840 dollars that you paid in interest.

Now instead of paying just 20 dollars a month, what if you pay 10 dollars over the minimum, or 30 dollars a month? Will that extra 10 dollars per month make any real difference? The answer is *YES*. Why?

Because after you have paid all the interest charges for the month, 15 dollars will be applied toward the principal that you owe. Now you will pay off your credit card not in 92 months but in just 45 months. Yes, in less than four years, you will have a zero balance on your credit card. You have cut the time it takes to pay off your card by more than half! All this happened because you paid 10 dollars more than the minimum due each month. In addition to paying off your credit card much sooner, when you pay $10 over the minimum due, you will have paid a total of just $1,350, or just 350 dollars in interest. That is almost a 500-dollar savings!

So whenever possible, never pay just the minimum due on a credit card. Always pay at least ten dollars over the minimum amount each month. If you can pay more than ten dollars over the minimum amount, do it.

Earn a Guaranteed 18 Percent

Say you have some money that you want to invest. But like most people, you also have credit card balances for which you are charged 1.5 percent a month interest, or 18 percent annually. What should you do with your money? The answer is to pay off your credit cards! Why earn 8 percent on an investment when you are paying 18 percent on your credit cards? You are not making money, you're losing money. You are losing 10 percent when you have a guaranteed way to earn 18 percent on your money.

Pay off your credit cards and stop paying 18 percent interest!

Take Advantage of Debit Cards

To keep your credit card balances low, whenever possible use a debit card instead of a credit card. You have to have money in your account to use a debit card, but debit cards have some major advantages. Because you are using your own money to instantly pay for things, you are not incurring debt that you will have to pay back, nor do you have to pay any interest charges. Using your debit card is a lot safer than using cash, and as long as you have enough money in your account, you can make the purchase you want without worrying whether you have enough cash in your wallet or purse.

Do You Need Overdraft Protection?

Many people still use checks and also have money automatically taken out of their account, such as their vehicle payment. For these reasons and others, it is possible to not have enough money in your account. Unless you have arranged for overdraft protection, checks can bounce, and you can be charged fees for not having enough money in your account. These fees can be substantial. But with overdraft protection, you are not charged any insufficient-funds fees. Your overdraft protection will automatically kick in to prevent anything from bouncing. Everyone should make arrangements with their bank to have overdraft protection. It costs nothing to arrange overdraft protection, so do it.

CHAPTER 5

Balancing Your Checkbook

It is a good idea to balance your checkbook (or bank account) each month. You may find that money is coming out of your account without your permission. Or you may find that you forgot to record a check that you wrote and you activated your overdraft protection. But many people do not balance their checkbook because they do not know how to do it. So I am going to explain a very easy method.

Every month, you get a statement from your bank, either online or in the regular mail. You need this statement to balance your bank account. Suppose this is the statement you received from your bank:

Date of Statement: May 28, 2015
Beginning Balance: $1,286.15
Deposits: $4,261.12

Charges against your account: $4,117.43 (including an electronic funds transfer for your car loan of $250.)
Monthly Service Charge: $5.00
Ending Balance: $1,424.84
Your checkbook on June 2, 2015, shows a balance of $3,810.40.

Please notice that your checkbook balance is much higher than what the bank shows as your balance. No need to worry, you have not started to balance your checkbook yet.

Balance your checkbook by using my check-check method. If an item is on both the bank statement and your checkbook register, then forget about it because both you and the bank know about the transaction. You are looking for two things: the first is what the bank does not know. The second is what you do not know.

Start with what the bank does not know. Your statement date is May 28, 2015. You got paid $2,130.56 on May 29. This is not reflected on your bank statement because it happened after the bank statement was sent to you. So you have to take the bank ending balance of $1,424.84 and add $2,130.56 to it, leaving you a new bank balance of $3,555.40.

Now go to what *you* do not know. Because your car payment of $250 happens automatically each month, you forgot to deduct it. So take your bank balance of $3,810.40 and subtract $250. This leaves you with a balance of $3,560.40. You also did not subtract the $5 bank service charge. When you subtract $5 from $3,560.40, you get $3,555.40.

You will notice that the new bank balance and your check register balance are the same: $3,555.40. You have just balanced your checkbook.

That was a very easy example. If you still write checks, it is possible that some outstanding checks had not cleared the bank by the time of your bank statement. If that is the case and you discovered it with my check-check method, you would simply subtract the amount of any outstanding checks from your bank statement.

The Benefits of Direct Deposit

Some banks have a cutoff time of 2:00 p.m. If you are in the bank after that time, your transaction will not register until the next business day. Well, most people are paid on a Friday. If you get to the bank after 2:00 p.m. on Friday, it's like you are really at the bank on Monday. If you wanted access to all your money this weekend, it's not going to happen. This could really be a downer for your weekend plans. One way to prevent this is to get direct deposit. Your paycheck is automatically deposited into your account. You can be paid on Friday and get something to eat and drink on Friday morning, and fill up your car with gas on the way to work. No going to work, getting your check, and having to get to the bank to deposit your paycheck. The money is already in your account when you wake up Friday morning. It costs nothing to arrange direct deposit of your paycheck with your bank. It not only saves you time, it also gives you access to your money sooner. Since it costs nothing to arrange direct deposit, you should do it.

CHAPTER 6

Getting Some Wheels

Unless you are into yachts, a vehicle is the second-most-expensive item you will purchase in your life, with a house being number one. You can save a lot of money if you follow the advice in this book. If you want to purchase a new vehicle, the first thing you have to do is join a credit union. Once you're a member of a credit union, you can use their car-buying service, at no cost to you. You tell the credit union the make, model, and features you want on your vehicle, and you can even request the color. I did this less than a year ago, and I paid three thousand dollars less than the invoice price. The invoice price is different from the sticker price on the car's window. You can save thousands of dollars like I did. You might be asking, how is that possible? The answer is knowing that the invoice price you see is not the real invoice price. The first invoice price assumes that the car dealership purchases the cars on the lot one at a time. But that is not the case. It purchases them by the truckload, so it gets the fleet price from Honda or Ford or whomever the manufacturer is.

A credit union can also save you money on the financing of your new vehicle. Financing through the dealership or a bank can be very expensive. Credit unions exist for the benefit of their members. So the rates are lower, much lower than at the banks. And this can save you thousands of dollars in interest charges. You can also save money by shopping the loan interest rate to see who has the lowest rate.

Don't add insurance on the loan. If you own personal life insurance and you die, your beneficiary can use the proceeds from your life insurance policy to pay off the loan on your car. And the cost of the life insurance policy that you have is going to be a lot less than the cost of the insurance from the dealership.

Many people who are looking to purchase a vehicle already have a vehicle. Kelly Blue Book (www.kbb.com) can tell you what your vehicle is worth. If you want to trade in your vehicle, it is very important to know what it's worth, so you can get a good price and not get ripped off. Always do your homework. And knowing what your vehicle is worth is part of doing your homework.

Should You Lease or Purchase?

If you have a job as an insurance agent or real estate agent, or another job where you use your vehicle for work, it makes sense to lease a vehicle. But for most people, purchasing is the smarter option. When you lease a vehicle, you have to turn the vehicle in at the end of the lease period. You have no trade-in, so most people end up leasing another vehicle. Yes, leasing a vehicle is a little cheaper each month than buying, but I will show that in the long run, owning will save you a lot more money.

When you lease a vehicle, you can only drive it so far, usually 1,000 miles a month. That means if you have a three-year lease, you can only drive 36,000 miles. But what if you drive more than 36,000 miles? Depending on your lease, you will owe the leasing company 10 cents to 25 cents a mile for every mile over 36,000 miles! If you drive 1,000 miles over 36,000 miles, at 25 cents a mile, you would owe the lease company an extra 250 dollars. I know people who do not drive their car near the end of the lease because if they did, they would owe the leasing company even more money, so the car just sits in the driveway. But this is just one of many reasons why purchasing a vehicle is the best option for most people in the long run.

If you lease a car, the odds are you will lease another car when your lease ends, and your payments will just go on and on. But if you purchase a car, your payments will end. You might have a three-year, four-year, five-year, or six-year loan. But at the end of that time, you own the car. Your monthly payments will end! Not only do you own your car, you can keep your car as long as you want and will not have a monthly car payment. If you decide to get a new car, you can use your existing car as your down payment. The biggest advantage of owning versus leasing is the period of time you can go without a monthly car payment. This can be years. You can have a three-year car loan, make all thirty-six monthly payments, then keep your car another six years or longer. You can't do this when you lease one car after another. This advantage of not having to make a monthly car payment will add up to thousands of dollars saved each year.

The Importance of a Good Credit Rating

Having a good credit rating will help you get approved for a car loan and get the lowest interest rate that is being offered. You have probably seen car commercials offering 0 percent or 0.9 percent financing. But those rates are only available to customers with the best credit ratings. The same is true with getting a mortgage. So follow all the suggestions in this book, and you will have a great credit rating and will be the one who gets the lowest possible rate.

Buying a Rental Car

Rental-car companies get new cars every year. When they get their new cars, they sell their existing cars. Most of the cars they sell have less than ten thousand miles on them. A car that costs eighteen thousand dollars new can be purchased in the ten-thousand- to twelve-thousand-dollar range, depending on the make, options on the car, and miles driven. You can get the car for a lot less due to depreciation, the lower value due to normal wear and tear. The more miles a car has been driven, the more depreciation, and thus the lower resale price.

So if you are looking to get a car, one option is to purchase a car from a rental-car agency. The car you purchase should be only a year old, might have less than ten thousand miles on it, and the price should be thousands less than if you purchased the car new.

Cars That Have Been Leased

Approximately 50 percent of the cars on the road in America have been purchased, and about 50 percent are leased. Most lease periods are two or three years. What percentage of people keep their leased car after the lease period ends? One percent! Yes, 99 percent of people who lease turn in their leased car at the end of the lease period. What do the people who turned in a leased car do? They lease another car, a new car with all the new bells and whistles on it.

So what happens to the cars that people gave back to the dealership when their lease ended? Those cars go on the used car lot to be resold. With 50 percent of cars being leased and 99 percent of those cars ending up on the used car lot, there are a ton of previously leased cars for sale. So you will find vehicles of every make and model to choose from.

This creates a buyer's market. You can select the make, model, and features you want and can even wait for the color you want. And you will not have to wait long. Plus, most of those previously leased cars are still under warranty. Once again, because of deprecation, the previously leased cars will sell for thousands less than a new car. You can get the car you want for 20 to 25 percent less than the cost of the car if it was new. This means that if the car cost twenty thousand dollars new, it's possible to get it after it has been leased for two or three years in the fifteen-thousand-dollar to sixteen-thousand-dollar range, depending on the length of the lease, the model, and the options and features on the car. And you can even get a car under warranty in many cases. You will also have a substantially lower monthly car payment when you purchase a car that has been leased.

But there are even more advantages. When you purchase a car that has been leased, your auto insurance will cost less because the car is used. Another advantage is that your monthly car payments will eventually end, and you will own the car outright. You can keep the car with no monthly payments. You can also trade your car in when you purchase another car, so you don't have to come up with a cash down payment. You also are not forced to get a new leased car because you do not have either a cash down payment or a trade-in. You now have many options.

Buy a Car with Cash

I am using the word *car*, but the word represents any kind of vehicle, including SUVs and trucks. I have already covered how to make a budget and that unless you use your car for business, you should purchase a car and not lease it. I have also covered purchasing a car from a rental car company or a car that has been leased. But the truth is that a lot of people want to purchase a new car. In case you are one of those people, I will show you a plan to get a new car without a car payment!

Most people keep a car for five or six years. I am going to ask you to keep your car six years. Many people get a five-year car loan, so let's say you have a five-year loan, and your monthly car payment is 250 dollars. Once you finish making the payments on your car, I want you to keep your budget unchanged. Take the 250 dollars a month that you were using to make your car payment and separate it into two parts: 50 dollars and 200 dollars. Take the 50 dollars a month and have fun with it. Spend it on something you really like. Enjoy yourself. Take the 200 dollars and put it in a savings account. Not counting interest, you will have 2,400 dollars at the end of the year.

My goal is to get you to have a three-year car loan and keep the car for six years. If you can go directly to a three-year car loan, great. If not, go with a four-year car loan, and then the next time, go with a three-year car loan. The best part is that the monthly payment on the four-year loan will be lower than that on your five-year loan! That's because you used your existing car as a trade-in and added the 2,400 dollars you saved during the sixth year you owned your car. Once the four-year car loan has ended, keep your car for two more years, putting 200 dollars a month in your savings account. Not counting interest, you will have 4,800 dollars in two years. Now trade in your car and use the 4,800 dollars to purchase your new car with a three-year car loan. Remember to go to www.kbb.com to make sure you are getting a good price on your trade-in.

Once the three-year car loan ends, continue to save 200 dollars a month for three years. That is 36 times that you put 200 dollars into your savings account. Not counting interest, you will have 7,200 dollars in your savings account at the end of three years. Now trade in your car and add your 7,200 to purchase a car for cash! That's right, no car payment!

Now put 150 dollars a month into your saving account each month, and take 50 dollars a month and just have fun with it. Yes, blow it on something you enjoy each month. At the end of six years, not counting interest, you will have 10,800 dollars in your savings account. You can trade in your car and also use the $10,800 to purchase your next car for cash!

The second-most-expensive thing you will pur-chase—a car—is now something you are buying with cash plus a trade-in. You also have an emergency fund for all the curveballs that life throws at you. You are well on your way to having your financial house in order. (This plan will work great until your child turns seventeen or eighteen and wants a car.)

Do You Need Rental-Car Insurance?

When many people go on vaca-tion, they fly to their destination. When they arrive, they need a car. When getting the rental car, you will be asked if you want to purchase insurance on the rental car. Always turn down this insurance, no matter how many times you are asked to purchase it. Why? Because if you get into an accident in your rental car, the first thing the rental-car com-pany will tell you is to contact the insurance carrier that you have for your car at home. That is the primary coverage. The coverage that you get on the rental car, in some cases at a cost of more than ten dollars a day is secondary and rarely if ever is used. Yes, you are paying ten dollars a day or more for something you will never use, so save your money and don't purchase the coverage. At ten dollars a day for a seven-day vacation, you will save seventy dollars on each vacation you take from now on! What many people fail to realize is that the coverage you have is on you, not the car! Let's say your neighbor, a friend of yours, picks you up in his car and you go somewhere. On the way home, your neighbor falls ill and asks you to drive his car home. So you do. When you are driving your neighbor's car, you have insurance coverage. Why? Because the coverage you have with your auto insurance carrier is on you, not your car. The same logic holds when you are driving a rental car on vacation. You already have coverage, so you don't need to purchase it for a second time. Save your money.

CHAPTER 7

Buying a House

This book has already told you how to save money on your car, the second-most-expensive thing you will likely ever purchase. It is now time to save you money on the most expensive thing you will purchase: a house.

First-Time Home-Buyer Programs

Each state has a first-time home-buyer program designed to transform people from renters to homeowners. The benefits vary from state to state, but you can get help with closing costs, a lower interest rate on your mortgage and more, so it is definitely worth checking out.

How many times can you be a first-time home buyer? The obvious answer is once. But the correct answer could be fifty-one times! Purchasing a house in Maryland might not exclude you from being a first-time home buyer in another state. So if you have moved and now live in another state or the District of Columbia, and you have not purchased a house in that state, you should see if you qualify. To your surprise, you might.

ARMs Versus Thirty-Year Fixed Mortgages

An ARM is an adjustable rate mortgage. The rate adjusts each year based on what has happened to interest rates during the year. ARMs start at a lower rate than thirty-year fixed mortgages. But unless rates really drop in the first year of your mortgage, the ARM will go up at the end of your first year. Most adjustable rate mortgages are two-six ARMs. That means they can go up 2 percent a year and go up a total of 6 percent over the life of the loan. So for example, if your ARM starts at 3 percent, it could go as high as 9 percent! Yes, your interest rate could triple in just a few years!

Thirty-year fixed-rate mortgages are exactly what they sound like. Their rate will remain fixed for thirty years. But that does not mean your mortgage payment will remain fixed? Your mortgage payment includes the following: the principal and interest on your mortgage, your homeowner's insurance, and your property taxes. Over time, property taxes can and do go up. Unless you make arrangements to pay this increase separately, your mortgage payment will go up.

You need to pay attention to interest rates. Even if you got a thirty-year fixed mortgage, if rates drop enough, it might make sense to refinance and lock in a lower rate. That means a lower monthly mortgage payment. The same is true with an ARM. You can lock in a low rate or refinance with an ARM just like you can with a thirty-year fixed mortgage. It is not uncommon for people to refinance at a lower rate and save hundreds on their monthly mortgage payment. Over the course of a thirty-year mortgage, that will add up to thousands of dollars saved.

Fifteen-Year Versus Thirty-Year Mortgage

A fifteen-year mortgage costs more per month than a thirty-year mortgage for the same mortgage amount. But because you finish making payments fifteen years sooner, a fifteen-year mortgage will save you thousands of dollars over a thirty-year mortgage. In many cases, it will save you more than one hundred thousand dollars, depending on the size of the mortgage and the interest rate. So if you can afford a fifteen-year mortgage, get it.

Many people can't afford a fifteen-year mortgage and have to get a thirty-year mortgage. If you have a thirty-year mortgage, I will cover two plans to help you save money.

Plan One: Paying Half Your Mortgage Payment Every Two Weeks

There are fifty-two weeks in a year. Since you will be making half a mortgage payment every two weeks, divide fifty-two in half and you get twenty-six. When you make twenty-six half-mortgage payments, that is the equivalent to making thirteen full mortgage payments, or an extra full mortgage payment each year. This extra mortgage payment each year will cut seven to eight years off your thirty-year mortgage! Yes, you could be finished in twenty-two years instead of thirty years. There are companies that try to sell you this plan, but you can make arrangements with your existing mortgage company to do this for free. Just contact your mortgage company, and they will set it up for you.

Plan Two: Paying Extra on the Principal

Most people get paid once every two weeks, so you may get twenty-six paychecks a year. Your budget is set up for two paychecks a month, or twenty-four paychecks. Two months out of twelve, you will get three paychecks in one month. You have budgeted for two paychecks, so twice a year you get an extra paycheck!

In the first seven years of a thirty-year mortgage, almost 99 percent of your payment goes to pay interest, not principal. So your mortgage balance goes down very little over this period.

What I want you to do is when you have an extra paycheck, pay half of a mortgage payment to be applied directly to the principal balance. When you send in this extra money, make sure to tell your mortgage company to apply it to the principal on your loan. Type out a note, and include it with your payment. You will do this twice a year, paying the same amount as one full mortgage payment directly to the principal on your mortgage. A few days after mailing the extra money to your mortgage company, call the company to make sure the money is applied directly to the principal on your mortgage, as you instructed them. This will cut fourteen to fifteen years off your mortgage! Yes, you can turn a thirty-year mortgage into a fifteen-year mortgage!

Life is full of curveballs. You never know in advance when one is going to hit you. If you get hit with a financial curveball and you need the extra money you were going to pay on the principal of your mortgage, use the money for your financial curveball. Hopefully, I have gotten you to establish an emergency fund, and you could use your emergency fund to deal with your financial emergency, so you could still pay the extra on your principal. The plan is to get you to save those fourteen or fifteen years of mortgage payments and save over one hundred thousand dollars!

Increase Your Tax Deductions

When I purchased my first house, I was "house poor" and eating hot dogs because that was the only food I could afford. Then I did my federal and state income taxes and received a combined refund of over 5,000 dollars. It was at that moment that I realized my mistake. I was a single guy, and I had not increased my deductions. I went into work the next day and increased my deductions. My take-home pay went up by more than 350 dollars a month. I now had money to purchase food other than hot dogs. The interest you pay on your mortgage payments and the property taxes you pay are deductible on your federal and state income taxes. So learn from my mistake. No sense struggling all year just to pay your bills and eat, and then get a big federal and state refund. Increase your deductions if you just purchased your first house. Get that money in your paycheck now, and put that money toward some bills and some necessities, such as food. In the year that you purchase a house, you get some write-offs. The deductions have changed, and you might not save as much as I did because of these changes, but the concept still holds.

An Exception

You have to be honest with yourself. Are you a person who will always spend all the money in your wallet or purse, no matter how much money you started with? If this is you, you might not want to increase your deductions. Your tax refund may be the only way to save enough money to go on vacation. Yes, the government is taking money out of your pay and holding it at 0 percent interest for more than a year before you file your taxes and get your refund. It's not a good deal, but if you have trouble saving money, it might be the only way you can save enough for a vacation or other large purchases.

I started this section by asking you to be honest with yourself. I will describe a much better situation, then you will have to be honest when answering a question.

Have 25 to 50 dollars per pay period taken out of your pay and sent via EFT directly to a savings account with your bank, savings and loan, or credit union. This money will not show up in your checkbook balance, wallet, or purse. You now have access to this money all year long, and it will earn some interest. The money can be used as an emergency fund for all of life's curveballs that get thrown at you. It can also be used to go on vacation or for other large purchases.

Now the question: you know this money is being taken out of your pay each pay period. Once a month, you will receive a statement from your financial institution showing your balance. Will you withdraw this money, just to have it? If you are honest with yourself and answered yes, then this plan will not work for you. It is only a matter of time before you take the money that you have saved up and blow it. You are a person who has to get a big tax refund to save over one thousand dollars.

If you answered the question with a no, then this plan will work for you. It is better than getting a big refund each year because you have access to your money, and you earn some interest as well.

Owning Versus Renting

If you rent an apartment, you are not building any equity. Each month, you pay your rent to keep the right to live where you are. But you get no other benefit from your money. Owning a condo, town house, or single-family house has major advantages over renting. As mentioned earlier, when you file your taxes, you can deduct the interest you pay on your mortgage as well as the property taxes you pay. But owning can also have another financial benefit: appreciation. The condo, town house, or house that you purchase can go up in value. Yes, we have had periods when the housing bubble has burst and house values have declined, but for the vast majority of the time, housing prices have continued to go up. If you are a homeowner, you will benefit from this increase in housing prices.

Owning for Less than Renting

For a long time, interest rates have remained low. It is possible that you can own a condo, town house, or single-family house for less than the cost of renting. If owning has the advantages of tax write-offs and potential increases in the value of your house, and it costs less than renting, why do so many people still rent? There are two primary reasons: bad credit and the down payment.

If you have bad credit, it is not something you have to live with your entire life. Everyone can change his or her credit score. Pay your bills on time. Always pay the minimum amount on your credit cards and hopefully at least ten dollars more than the minimum. Keep these practices up, and over time your credit score will improve. Follow the advice in this book. Build an emergency fund. Join a credit union. Credit unions usually offer better rates on car loans or debt-consolidation loans than a bank. Even if you have had to declare bankruptcy in the past, it is not something that will ruin your credit forever. Every month that you follow the advice in this book, your credit score will continue to improve.

The biggest reason people continue to rent instead of own is that they have not saved up enough for the down payment on a house. Many people live paycheck to paycheck with no plan. At the end of the year, they do not know where all their money went. In most cases, you only need to save up for a down payment once in your lifetime. Why? Because when you sell your current house, you can use the proceeds from that sale for the down payment on your next house.

How badly do you want to own instead of rent? Are you willing to give up a vacation, not eat out as often, and buy fewer shoes and video games until after you own your house? If you have the mindset that nothing is going to stop you from owning your own place, nothing will stop you! Contact the first-time home-buyer's program for your state. Talk to a real estate agent and find out how big a mortgage can you qualify for. Accompany a real estate agent to visit some homes that you could realistically afford until you see some that you like. How much do they cost? What would your down payment have to be to purchase one of those homes? That amount becomes your savings goal. If you want it bad enough, you will find a way to save that amount over the next few years to make your goal of homeownership a reality. And don't be afraid to think outside the box. For example, renting to own is when your rent is used as part of your down payment. You also might be able to get a 100 percent financing loan, so you do not have to come up with a down payment to purchase a house.

On a personal note, I was living in New Jersey and working in New York City, in the financial services industry, when I bought my first home. I had two options: to rent an apartment in New York City or purchase a house in New Jersey, in the Oranges. The rent and the mortgage payment were about the same. I purchased the house, and in seven years I sold the house for a seventy-five-thousand-dollar gain. Had I rented an apartment in New York City, I would have had nothing to sell and would have had no gain at all. I also got all those write-offs on my taxes for the interest payments and property taxes over the seven years. So I came out way ahead. You will too. Also, once in your lifetime, after you turn fifty-five years old, you can sell a house and keep all the profits and pay no taxes on the gain. If you rent all your life, you will not have anything to sell. So make it a goal in life to own a condo, town house, or single-family home.

CHAPTER 8

Investing in Mutual Funds

What is a mutual fund? As CNN Money describes it, "A mutual fund pools money from hundreds and thousands of investors to construct a portfolio of stocks, bonds, real estate, or other securities, according to its charter. Each investor in the fund gets a slice of the total pie. The money is then invested by a team of professionals, who research stocks, bonds or other assets and then place the money as wisely as they can." You get professional direction and instant diversification.

I am sure you have heard the saying "Don't put all your eggs in one basket." This expression is telling you that it is a smart move to diversify when you invest. This is exactly what you are doing with a mutual fund. A stock mutual fund, for example, will usually contain more than twenty stocks, and often more than thirty stocks. Compare this to owning just one stock and purchasing more and more shares of that one stock. The more diversified you are, the less risk you are taking.

Let's say you want to invest in stocks that are in the technology field. The portfolio manager who runs your technology mutual fund is an expert in the technology field. The manager will choose the best technology stocks he or she can for the fund. While you are working and living your life, the fund manager is staying current in the technology field and managing the fund's portfolio.

A Disclaimer

> Mutual funds do involve risk. You can lose some or all of your principal. But mutual funds have many advantages, including professional management, diversification, and a stated objective of the fund.

What's Your Plan?

When you invest in a mutual fund, you should have a plan. It might be to invest in stocks, bonds or real estate, or in something else. But just saying you want to invest in stocks is not enough. What kind of stocks? Do you want to specialize in an industry such as technology or telecommunications? Or do you want large-company stocks or midsize-company stocks? Do you want stocks that have a history of paying a high dividend? Value stocks? Growth stocks? The list goes on and on, and mutual funds for each type of stock mentioned above do exist.

Risk and Your Risk Tolerance

Unlike parking your money in a fixed-rate savings account or a certificate of deposit, you run the risk of losing some money with mutual funds. They are not guaranteed to go up. It is not uncommon for the stock market to have a great day on Monday, followed by a bad day on Tuesday, or vice versa. The question is, can you handle the roller-coaster ride?

If the possibility of the market having a bad day is going to keep you up at night worrying, then you should not be in mutual funds. You have to be comfortable with the risk you are taking. You need to have the mindset of making a long-term investment. Mutual funds should not be purchased, in my opinion, on Monday and sold for a huge profit on Wednesday, just two days later. I am not saying that can't happen; what I am saying is that your goal in purchasing a mutual fund should be long term.

I have asked you previously in this book to be honest with yourself. I am now going to ask you to be honest with yourself again.

What kind of person are you when it comes to risk and your investments? Are you willing to risk some or all of your principal for a potentially higher rate of return than you can get at a bank in a fixed savings account?

When driving your vehicle, when do you normally go to the gas station to fill up? When the tank is three-fourths full? One-half full? Less than one-half full? One-fourths full? Or when the tank is almost on empty?

The closer to empty your vehicle is before you normally go to the gas station to fill up, the more of a risk taker you are. All mutual funds do not contain the same amount of risk. You should read the prospectus of a mutual fund that you are considering. Most mutual-fund companies will tell you where the fund falls on the risk spectrum. If you are not told, be sure to ask before investing any money in that mutual fund.

A Ready-Made Portfolio

Many people like to purchase stocks, one company at a time. But when you purchase a mutual fund, you are buying into a portfolio of more than twenty stocks, all with a common goal. This is much different from building your portfolio one stock at a time. When you purchase a mutual fund, you get an instant portfolio. It is the fund manager's job, not yours, to manage that portfolio. So buying a mutual fund is in many ways the opposite of building and managing your own portfolio.

Income-Producing Stocks

Income-producing stocks are stocks that have a history of paying a high dividend. Once a company has declared a dividend, it is extremely difficult to cut the dividend. Why? Because as soon as a company cuts its dividend, everyone thinks that something is wrong with the company. The stock price will almost always drop significantly when a company lowers its dividend. In addition to watching the stock price drop, the company will also anger its existing stockholders. So companies rarely if ever lower a stock's dividend, and stock dividends remain very stable.

From time to time, a company will raise the stock dividend. But companies are very reluctant to raise their dividend because they know they will not be able to lower it in the future without negative consequences. So if a company has a long history of paying a 4 percent dividend, it will most likely continue to pay that dividend. With interest rates being very low, getting 4 percent on your money is much more than banks are paying in interest on savings accounts.

But 4 percent is not the only return you can get from owning a stock that pays a high dividend. The stock can also go up. So you have both the dividend return and the potential for the stock to appreciate. If, for example, a stock pays a 4 percent dividend and also goes up 6 percent during the year, you make a total of 10 percent on your investment. Of course, the stock price can also go down.

Where can you find stocks that have a history of paying a high dividend? In a mutual fund called an equity-income fund.

No-Load Versus Loaded Mutual Funds

Mutual funds come in two types: loaded mutual funds and no-load mutual funds. If you have a loaded mutual fund, a percentage is taken out of every dollar invested. For example, if you have a 6 percent loaded mutual fund, then six cents out of every dollar invested is subtracted, and only 94 cents out of every dollar goes into the fund. If you invest in a no-load mutual fund, 100 percent of every dollar is put into the fund. Each year, a percentage of the fund's return is subtracted to pay management fees. For example, if the no-load mutual fund you invested in earns 13.5%, a 1.5% management fee may be subtracted and you are left with a return of 12 percent. Vanguard, Fidelity, and T. Rowe Price are the three largest no-load mutual fund companies.

Earnings Season

After each calendar quarter ends, each company on the New York Stock Exchange, Nasdaq, and the American Stock Exchange reports its earnings for the quarter. So January, April, July, and October are the four months out of the year known as earnings season. Why is this important? Experts on Wall Street determine what each company's profits per share should be. If a company misses that target and earnings per share are lower than predicted, even by just one cent per share, the stock of that company can drop by 20 percent or more in one day. Because millions of shares are outstanding, missing by one cent per share means missing by a very large amount, and things are far worse than what was predicted.

The goal is to "beat the street": to beat Wall Street's estimate of the company's earnings. If a company can do that, even by one cent per share, then the price of that stock may rise by 20 percent or more in a single day.

What happens if a company's earnings per share come in exactly as predicted? Then the stock price remains the same. Unless this happens, a company's stock price will shoot way up or fall way down. That is why earnings season is so important. If you own a mutual fund, the stocks in the mutual fund's portfolio will be greatly affected by earnings season. If the majority of the stocks in the mutual fund beat the street, the share value of that mutual fund will rise. The opposite is true if the majority of the companies in the mutual fund fail to meet their earnings estimates.

A Paper Loss Versus a Real Loss

Many people do not understand the difference between a paper loss and a real loss. Knowing the difference can save you thousands of dollars. Suppose you purchase one hundred shares of Stock X at one hundred dollars a share. The day after you purchase Stock X, the stock price drops to ninety dollars a share. How much money have you lost? The correct answer is zero dollars! You have lost nothing! You have what is called a paper loss of one thousand dollars. But you still own your one hundred shares of Stock X. If you sell all your shares of Stock X at ninety dollars a share, you turn a paper loss into a real loss.

Now let's suppose that the price of Stock X goes up to 120 dollars a share. How much money have you made? Again, the answer is zero dollars! You have a paper gain of 2,000 dollars. If you sell all your Stock X shares at the 120 dollars per share price, then you turn a paper gain into a real gain of 2,000 dollars. If you do nothing, all you have is a gain on paper.

You must take action and sell to turn a paper gain into a real gain, or a paper loss into a real loss. Many people look online, see that the price of a stock they own has gone down, and think that they have lost money. That is wrong. All they have is a paper loss. The stock market changes every business day. It can be down today and up tomorrow, or vice versa. You can have a paper loss on Monday and have a paper gain the very next business day. The secret is to not panic and sell your stock the minute it has a paper loss. If you do that, you will always be turning a paper loss into a real loss.

Pension Plans

Millions of people have retirement plans, and each month, billions of dollars are invested in them. Some companies have a matching program where if the employee puts in, say, 3 percent, and the company will match 3 percent dollar for dollar or fifty cents on the dollar. So in some cases it is not just the employee's money that is being invested but money from the company as well. The question is: where is this retirement money being invested? The answer is mutual funds. They can be fixed accounts, bond funds, stock funds, or other options.

In most cases, once you arrange to have this money taken out of your pay and invested, it will keep coming out of your pay automatically, unless you take action to stop it. The big benefit here is the automatic feature. On the first and the fifteenth of each month or every other Friday, depending on how you get paid, this money is automatically taken out and invested in the mutual fund options you have selected. This money is called qualified money because it is part of a qualified pension plan. If course, nonqualified money (money not from a qualified pension plan) goes into mutual funds each month as well.

Standard and Poor's 500-Stock Index

Diversification is a very good thing. By investing in an S&P 500 fund, you are investing in the country's largest 500 companies. A computer divides up your money so you get the proper diversification. The S&P 500 is an unmanaged index, and the management fees on an S&P 500 fund are low. Almost every pension plan has the S&P 500 index as an investment option. For this reason, it is a very large mutual fund. When the nightly news reports how the stock market did for that day, it almost always includes the results of the S&P 500.

I believe that if you are going to invest in stock mutual funds, some of your money should be put into the S&P 500. The stock market is going to have times when it is doing well (a bull market) and times when it is not doing well (a bear market), and while investing in stocks is risky, I believe that investing in the S&P 500 is less risky due to diversification. If you are investing in the S&P 500 as part of your pension plan, you are also dollar-cost averaging, which is discussed in the next section.

Dollar-Cost Averaging

When you invest the same dollar amount at regular intervals and purchase as many shares as that money can obtain, you are dollar-cost averaging. Paying fifty dollars every two weeks and getting as many shares as that fifty dollars will get you is an example. Dollar-cost averaging has some major advantages. As the price of the stock (or mutual fund) rises, you purchase fewer shares. As the price of the stock (or mutual fund) falls, you purchase more shares. This results in a lower average cost per share. The following example is exaggerated on purpose to illustrate this point.

The first investor on January 2 invests 1,200 dollars and receives 48 shares of a stock selling for 25 dollars a share. This investor is not dollar-cost averaging and makes no further purchases of the stock for the rest of the year.

The second investor buys 100 dollars of the same stock at the beginning of each month for 12 consecutive months, for a total of 1,200 dollars. As you can see, both investors are investing the same amount of money in the same stock over the same year.

In the first month, the stock sells for 25 dollars a share. After the first month, the stock price drops to 10 dollars a share. For months two through 11, the price remains at 10 dollars a share. For the 12th month, the stock rises to 20 dollars a share. At the end of one year, investor two has 109 shares—four shares purchased in the first month, 10 shares per month purchased over the next 10, months and five shares in the last month.

At the end of the year, investor one's stock is only worth $960 (48 x $20) for a paper loss of $240. Investor two's stock is worth $2,180 (109 x $20) for a paper gain of $980! How is this possible? The answer is the average price per share. Investor one's average price per share is $25, and the stock is only worth $20 at the end of the year. Investor two's average price per share is $11.01 ($1,200 divided by 109 shares), and the stock is selling for $20 at the end of the year.

Dollar-cost averaging has another advantage. Due to the lower average cost per share, and by purchasing more shares when the price falls, it is possible that the smaller investor, who does not have $1,200 at the start of the year but has $100 a month, each month, can outperform the larger investor by the end of the year.

If you are participating in your company's 401(k) or other type of pension plan on a bimonthly or monthly basis, you are dollar-cost averaging.

Unless you change the amount you are contributing to your pension plan each month, that amount will remain the same. And due to the automatic feature, it will continue to automatically be invested.

The stock market fluctuates every business day, so sometimes when the stock or mutual fund price has risen since your last purchase, you will purchase fewer shares, and when the stock or mutual fund price has fallen since your last purchase, you will purchase more shares. But as this process of rising and falling prices continues, you will lower your cost per share. Go back and look at the dollar-cost averaging example again. Notice that the price of the stock started out the year at $25 a share and ended the year at $20 a share. But the investor who dollar-cost averaged finished the year with a paper gain of $980! This is because his or her average cost per share was just $11.01 and the stock price was $20. As you can see from the example, the average price per share was the difference between a $980 paper gain for the investor who used dollar-cost averaging, and a $240 paper loss for the investor who did not use dollar-cost averaging.

CHAPTER 9

Understanding Bonds

The *Wall Street Journal* describes bonds as loans, or IOUs, where you serve as the bank. You loan your money to a company, a city, or the federal government—and that entity promises to pay you back in full, with regular interest payments.

If you buy a ten-year, one-thousand-dollar bond at 8 percent, you will get eighty dollars of interest each year for ten years, and at the end of the ten-year period, you will get your principal (your one thousand dollars) back. A secondary market exists if you want to sell your bond before the ten-year period has ended.

What Are the Risks with Bonds?

You have the risk that the company that you purchased the bond from might not pay you interest payments and also might not return your principal at maturity, or the end of the bond term. This is called *default risk.*

> But there are other risks. What happens if interest rates change after you purchase your bond? I will cover two possibilities. The first is that interest rates go up after you purchase your bond, and the second is that interest rates go down after you purchase your bond.
>
> 1) Suppose interest rates go up after you purchase your bond. You have a ten-year, 8 percent, one-thousand-dollar bond, and interest rates are now 10 percent. You can keep your bond and continue to get eighty percent interest a year. If you do this, you will notice that nothing has changed. If you want to sell your bond in the secondary market before maturity, however, you will be trying to sell an 8 percent bond in a 10 percent world. You will have to sell your bond at a discount, or a loss, so the person purchasing your bond gets 10 percent. By selling the bond below one

thousand dollars at nine hundred dollars,* the person who purchases your bond gets one thousand dollars at maturity, for a 10 percent return. Notice that as interest rates rose, the value of your bond went down.

2) Say interest rates go down after you purchase your bond. You have a 10-year, 8 percent bond, and interest rates are now 6 percent. The interest payments that you are getting on your bond (8 percent, or 80 dollars) are better than what new bonds are getting (6 percent, or 60 dollars). So if you want to sell your bond in the secondary marketplace, you can sell your bond for a premium, or more than 1,000 dollars. The person paying for your bond has to pay 1,100* dollars. Notice that as interest rates went down, the value of your bond went up.

*Numbers are for illustrative purposes only.

What has been described above is called *interest rate risk.* Interest rates might move in the wrong direction after you have purchased your bond, causing your bond to be worth less if you want to sell it in the secondary marketplace before maturity.

US government bonds are considered risk-free bonds. You have no fear of default because the United States can just print more money to pay off the bond. However, because you have no risk of default, the interest rate that the bond earns is low.

The Money Flow

The key to the money flow is interest rates. You will see from examples and a diagram that as the interest rate situation changes, so should your investment choices. For interest rates, let's use the three-year CD rate at a bank with FDIC insurance.

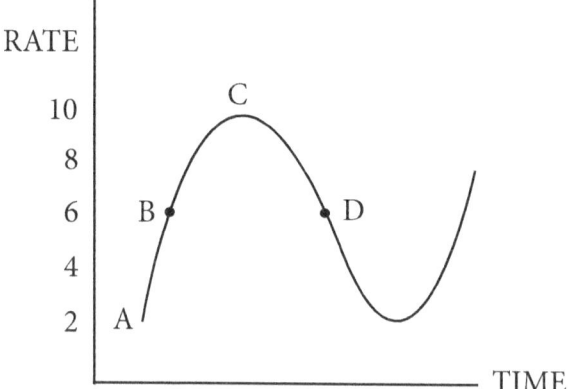

Start with the situation we have now, where interest rates are very low (point A on the diagram).

If you think interest rates might rise in the future, this is the wrong time to invest in bonds or a bond mutual fund. Why? Refer back to the bonds section. As interest rates rose, the value of the bond that you already owned went down in value. So what should you invest in, in a low interest-rate environment? The answer is the stock market and stock mutual funds. Investors have few other investments to choose from. So the money flows into the stock market and stock mutual funds, and they do very well during this period. Where else can an investor go to try to get a return of 8 percent or higher?

Now let's move to point B. In this example, rates are in the 5 percent to 6 percent range and approaching a transition point. Why? Because many senior citizens have a number in their head for fixed rates. I will explain.

Most people, as they age, become more conservative with their investments, especially retirement investments such as a pension plan. That is because they are closer to retirement. They can't take a huge paper loss just a few years before they plan to retire and start withdrawing their money.

What this means is if you offered people age fifty-five and older a fixed rate such as 10 percent, for example, many seniors would take that rate, jump out of the stock market, and lock in the 10 percent rate in a five-year certificate of deposit at a bank. Each senior has a number in his or her head. It might not be 10 percent; it might be 9 percent or even 8 percent. For some, it might even be 6 percent. So as interest rates start to approach 6 percent, you will start to see seniors take money out of the stock market and put it into fixed savings plans. The problem is that interest rates have not been that high in years, nor have they been anywhere close to those rates. Right now, banks are not even offering 3 percent on savings accounts. So many seniors are forced to invest in the stock market. Some are in equity-income funds, which invest in stocks that have a history of paying a high dividend. If interest rates were to approach 6 percent, stock market returns would start to suffer because investors would have alternatives.

When Interest Rates Are at or Near Their Peak

When interest rates have gone as high as you think they will go (point C), what should you do? If you refer back to the bonds section, as interest rates fell, the value of the bond that you owned went up in value. So when you think interest rates are at or near their peak, that is the time to purchase bonds. As interest rates fall more and more, the value of your bonds will continue to go up if you were to sell in the secondary marketplace or if you owned a bond mutual fund.

Now let's move to point D. This is a transition point. You can start to think about selling your bonds or bond mutual funds. As interest rates continue to fall, they will eventually get to where you think they are as low as they will go, so you should be getting back into the stock market.

CHAPTER 10

Deferred Annuities

Most people put money in a bank savings account. Even if you do not touch this money all year, you will get a statement from your bank telling you how much interest you earned, and you will have to report this interest income on your taxes. But if you put money into a deferred annuity and do not touch the money all year, you will not have to pay any interest income on your income taxes. This is a huge advantage. One disadvantage is that you might need a minimum of five thousand dollars. But if you have the minimum amount or more, a deferred annuity might be a savings option you should consider.

CHAPTER 11

Your Michael Jordan Moment

Most people know who Michael Jordan is. He is retired from the National Basketball Association and a member of the NBA Hall of Fame. Many people might not know that Michael Jordan made the winning shot in the National Championship game between the University of North Carolina and Georgetown University in 1982. Making that shot gave him the confidence that he could make any shot in the NBA. Confidence is the key. You need to have your Michael Jordan moment. It changed his life, and it will change your life. It does not have to have anything to do with sports.

I had my Michael Jordan moment in grad school. I graduated with my undergraduate degree on August 17. Eleven days later, I started an MBA program in finance. I was twenty-two years old and single. I was the baby of the class. The next-youngest person was twenty-eight years old. Most of the people in the program were in their thirties and married. Almost one-third of the class consisted of Japanese car executives from Honda, Toyota, and Mitsubishi. They were all male, and all they did was eat, sleep, and study. I was one of the few Americans who could beat them on the tests. I earned their respect, and I got the confidence that I could compete and win against anyone. That was my Michael Jordan moment: once I realized that I had the confidence to make A's in grad school and to graduate with honors.

You will have your Michael Jordan moment, and it will give you the confidence to do anything you set your mind to. And anything means anything. Believe you can do it, and you can. Having confidence is extremely important. Believe in yourself.

The Fear of the Unknown Is Worse than the Unknown

Many people do not do something because they are afraid. I have been afraid many times. But every time, the fear turned out to be worse than what I was afraid of. It can be something small or something big. What I was afraid of turned out to be not so bad. Recently I was afraid to use the videoconferencing app Zoom for the first time. It turned out Zoom was very easy to use.

Now, I have been afraid of some very big things. I am a finance teacher. The tech-education requirement in Maryland changed from Word, Excel, Access, and PowerPoint to engineering and the Inventor CAD software program. I had to go to Duke University in North Carolina over the summer. I didn't know one person, and not one thing about the Inventor CAD program. In two weeks, I had to learn everything I was going to teach for the upcoming school year, starting in August. Class was from 8:00 a.m. to 5:00 p.m. Then the homework took until 1:00 a.m. Yes, I was scared. But I had confidence, and I went to Duke and did it. And in just two years, I went the entire school year without a student asking me a question about the software that I did not know how to answer. Yes, I knew the software that well. I was scared big time as I drove to Duke University. But the software was not that bad. The fear was a lot worse than what I had to learn.

Don't let the fear in your life hold you back. Every time you face your fears, you will be glad you did. You don't have to do it alone. Rely on your support system You can and will succeed.

If You Have Nothing to Lose, Do It!

I mentioned this earlier in this book, but since it is my philosophy in life, and it has served me very well, I wanted to spend more time on it and give a few more examples on how it can help you. Many times in life, you will suffer a setback. You may have been late on a car payment or a credit card payment. Call up the credit card company and tell them that it was the first time that you were late. Ask them to waive the late fee. Since it is your first time you are late, they just might. The point is, if they say no, you are in the same situation that you are in now. So you have nothing to lose. Whenever you have nothing to lose, you should try. I have had many students who wanted to get into the University of Maryland. Since they are an instate resident, the University of Maryland gets a lot less money. Out of state students pay two to three times as much as an instate students. So getting into the University of Maryland as an instate student is very difficult. Many students received their rejection letter and told me as I was one of their teachers in high school. My advice was to not give up and to make an appointment with the University of Maryland and to go with their parents and try again. Many students who get accepted to the University of Maryland also got accepted to other universities like Georgetown or Princeton. They choose to go to one of those universities and not the University of Maryland. That leaves an opening at the University of Maryland. The student that did not give up and tried again many times gets a yes from the University of Maryland. If you live in a different state other than Maryland, just replace the university you want to attend in this example. The point, is even if you try again and get a no, what did you have to lose? The answer is nothing. So do it and try. Many times you will get good news.

In Summary

If you take the advice in this book, you will quickly get your financial house in order. You have learned how to avoid many pitfalls that thousands of people fall victim to. Put what you have learned into practice. Things can and will get better. But most importantly, you learned what you need to know without having to make the mistakes first!

About the Author

Michael D. A. Baker received his undergraduate degree and his MBA in corporate finance. He received his MBA at the age of twenty-three. He then spent fifteen years in the financial services industry, mostly in the New York City and Newark, New Jersey, area. While in New Jersey he got his master's in education from Seton Hall University. For the last twenty-one years he has been a high school teacher, teaching personal finance. He also spent more than ten years teaching college. He has received numerous awards both from the financial services industry and in his teaching career, and in May of 2021, he received the Maryland Financial Education and Capability Award for a high school teacher for the entire state of Maryland. He learned from his years in the financial services industry that most people never learned about finance in high school or college and thus have trouble in life with their finances. He wrote this book to help all those people who have trouble with their finances. Many of these people are living paycheck to paycheck. The Chinese have an old saying: a stupid person makes the same mistakes over and over again. A smart person learns from their mistakes, but a truly wise person learns from other people's mistakes. The goal of this book is to help you learn about personal finance without having to make the mistake first. Mr. Baker is married and lives in Maryland with his wife and daughters.